A
Hopeless
Romantic

Aaliyah Lane

Table of Contents

Left without a goodbye 4

Love Lost 6

Letting go 7

Walking Paradox 9

Soul Ties 11

Fire and Desire 14

You 16

The Aggravation 18

Luck Ran Up 19

Don't Slip or Let Go 20

Outside of the box 21

Nobody 23

In due time it will heal 24

Self-destruct 26

I can't do it 28

I just want to be close 30

Calamity 31

In a Daze 33

Going Insane 34

Colorful but Afflicted 36

I don't care 38

Time Out 39

Why? 40

Should I, or Should I Not? 42

Introduction:

Looking for love in all the wrong places, until I realized I needed to love myself first. I often wondered what love felt like while looking for it in another human. Someone to make me happy, appreciate me, and to cheer me on my accomplishments. I felt as if I could not be happy on my own. Becoming lost into my thoughts I turned obsessive over people who were only temporary which made me feel as if real love does not exist. I had to realize true love starts with loving yourself. In each poem I poured my heart and my soul out from past heartbreaks I felt as if I could never move on from. Instead, each poem reminds me how strong I am, how I was able to accomplish my dreams while communicating my past to others. Throughout the chaos, you can make a beautiful creation. Even within the calamity in my life, it was all for a purpose. Live and grow into your divine purpose.

Left without a goodbye

It's funny,

My dreams are better than reality.

Every now and then I see you,

And it's funny how all I want is you.

To kiss and hold you,

Just to see your face again.

Just to be in your presence again.

But it's pointless to think of that,

You left without a word.

Not even a warning was given.

I try to move on but,

It's you that I want.

But it's pointless to think that,

You left without a word.

Yeah it hurts,

To have a dream about being with someone

And then you wake up and they are not beside you.

To know they don't want anything to do with you anymore but,

You want to be a part of their lives,

I try to be with someone else but in the back of my mind is you.

Maybe I was in love and didn't even know,

Maybe I am still in love but can't show it.

I wonder if I will ever see you again,

I wonder if you will even care,

It's crazy how you treated me like nothing but,

It's just something about you that kept me holding on.

Just being around you made me smile,

Just hearing your voice made my heart warm up,

Just seeing your smile took away all the stress.

And your corny jokes that took my breath away,

They say everything happens for a reason,

But why did I meet you?

All I have is a broken heart with painful memories

That makes me want you even more.

I just wonder why you never said goodbye,

I'll dry my eyes but,

I just know they'll leak again,

I guess in this game of life,

I can never win.

Love Lost

So, let me get this straight,

You waste your time on the people you don't care about?

You do the minimum to keep in contact so that you still have a
way into their lives,

The worst thing in life is memories,

Flashbacks that come to haunt you,

Every song, every gesture,

Every scenery reminds me of you.

When you say things you won't do but,

Something happens and you don't follow through,

But is it true?

Do you even have a clue?

The pain you've put me through.

Open myself just a little and you get right through?

Every line I write all I see is you,

But what can I do?

Just move on and act like I don't know you like I use to.

Letting go

Why am I here?

In this room,

Just you and I,

It was wrong but felt so right,

Probably since I wasn't thinking clearly,

And the fact that your smile hypnotized me,

It was like you took advantage of me you see,

But when I finally sat down and thought about it,

I knew you were just a distraction,

Wobbly knees and a bright smile every time I see you.

But who would have knew,

My sunny days would turn blue,

Now, that I see you,

My mind goes from one thing to another.

My mind is in outer space,

And you are still stuck on earth.

And it hurts you know,

Because we can't get on the same page,

It's a shame.

How you continue to play games,

And the constant going back,

But I'm done.

I promise,

I'll close this chapter,

And I hope you have a happily ever after.

Walking Paradox

It's like I want you but,

I despise your ways,

But somehow, I think about you day to day,

But I just can't let myself be with you again,

I think about life in general,

Mostly memories,

Painful memories then I wonder why I'm sad,

Trying to be happy.

Sometimes I say things I don't mean,

Either out of anger or just to see what you will say,

Hiding my true feelings but by the way.

My feelings and thoughts change,

I'm a very confusing person.

Sometimes I want you close,

Then, far away.

I want your attention but,

Then again I don't.

Sometimes I want to walk up to you and say hi,

But I also just want to walk by and say nothing.

Yeah I'm a little shy, but also,

I'm very outgoing.

If someone said they fully understood me it's a lie,

Because I can barely understand myself,

One minute I love you,

Next minute I can't stand you,

Then a few minutes later,

I don't want to be bothered with you,

Sometimes I feel like talking, and most days I don't,

I'm constantly contradicting myself,

So if someone said they fully understood me it's a lie because,

I can barely understand myself.

I guess you can say I'm a walking paradox.

Soul Ties

Benefits with no ties,

Tell the truth with no lies,

hard to say, when you hold your feelings inside.

You shut yourself away as if I was the bad guy,

If you wanted benefits with no ties,

Then why are we soul ties?

You've been mentally gone for a minute,

My feelings for you grew deep, because I thought you was in it.

In it to win it, but your actions can't be forgiven.

Listen,

Everything about you was so tempting.

You wanted just the benefits but my body wouldn't listen.

You see, in a negative soul tie that's where the enemy lies,

Waiting to devour you in a nice disguise,

Thick thighs and nice eyes, but you don't realize the soul you entice,

Your soul is searching for someone to long for it just like mine is,

But in your lies, is where the enemy lives.

In your negative soul tie, it's not just something you had to physically give but it became your addiction and in the eyes of a human that is not good for you, your soul lives.

Now you're fighting the temptation, you're fighting to stay
alive,

But you go back to the negative soul tie and you actually die.

You die little by little, to the point no one recognizes you.

You die to yourself and you are becoming a monster you never
wanted to become,

All over one, soul tie.

One soul tie that you got yourself intertwined because you
believed the enemies lies,

You went off of a "good vibe", but you didn't realize what was
held inside.

Now you have a soul tie,

Because you believed the enemies lies.

Now it's hard to run away because the feelings you held inside.

But your attention is what my soul was craving,

My legs are shaking maybe we should stop for a minute,

I know we both say we just friends but there are somethings I
haven't mentioned,

I keep my feelings distant,

But a relationship is what I am reminiscing,

Maybe it will happen if I gave you a piece of me.

Maybe my heart will shatter if you ended up dissing me,

I'm sorry, I have to outweigh my options realistically.

I mean, everyone is doing it right?

My home girl does it all the time so I should be alright,

But what I didn't realize is that I opened up that door,

We connected once, then we did it some more.

Now I feel I'm falling in love but you're backing out.

The pain and sorrow makes me want to lash out,

But you think I'm just being "crazy",

And when I pick up on the things you do I consider it shady.

All over a soul tie,

A soul tie that lies that you don't even realize.

But I'm crazy, for noticing the little things.

The little things that changed me,

With the soul tie you gave me.

But we both did it,

It was fun while it lasted I admit it.

But the after effect backfired, and I feel I made a mistake.

But then I awake,

Awake from this soul tie and ask the Lord my soul to take.

I was tired of being run by a soul tie that I needed to break.

Fire and Desire

I came to the realization that you are a liar,

a compulsive liar,

you just want to chase after your own desires, but you don't see
the fire,

The fire of destruction,

The ultimate chaos,

In your desire,

The desire you have that will bring you to your biggest regret,

That should have been enough said.

But instead, you chose your own destiny.

You chose your own way and at the end,

You were left with nothing,

Drained of all of your essence,

All of your goodness to the wrong people.

Ah, I can only imagine.

It must have been so upsetting,

You thought it was for a good cause,

So you was willing to risk it all,

You was willing to put your dreams on pause,

For someone who saw all of your flaws,

But yet bruised you and knew about all of your scars,

Your scars that you have just healed from but exposed you like a fresh wound.

Someone who you loved so hard, was gone so soon,

Who you was infatuated with however,

You made every attempt to keep something that held no value to you,

They loved what you could provide but didn't care if you was deprived,

They played off of your emotions and left you depleted.

Someone who you wanted but to them you wasn't needed.

What we had was infinite,

My love had no boundaries.

You sacrificed true love,

For your counterfeit, who to you, was astonishing.

Well you made that decision,

Now it's the consequences you have to deal with,

All because you listened,

Listened to the wrong voice.

The fire in your desire became the loudest noise.

You

It's no use,

Because all I think about is you,

For some reason,

I long to see you again.

Every second,

Every minute,

Every hour,

I count down waiting to see you.

When I zone out of my mind,

I fantasize about you,

They say I want you because of your looks,

But your personality caught me.

It caught me like a baseball mitten,

Longing for more of your attention.

Like heaven sent,

You weren't perfect,

But somehow you felt worth it.

I should have picked up on discernment,

And tried to find where my mind went.

Because if it wasn't real,

Then why do I feel like this?

The thought of your lips giving me a kiss,

Like this,

This moment,

I've been waiting for a long time,

And we was just texting but we clicked,

But I can't try if I'm the only one putting in effort.

Ha, like you deserved it,

But it's just something about you,

Because even though it is hard to say,

But all I want is you.

The Aggravation

My heart longs for someone I can't have,

Do I become upset or ashamed?

But, I'm not the girl he has but had,

It is pointless,

But when I come to the realization,

I just need to mature a little,

I know what I deserve,

I know my worth,

I understand why it didn't work out,

And I realize why it couldn't be.

You didn't know how to treat me,

So, God made you flee,

Because it wasn't meant to be,

I search in the wrong areas,

And in all the wrong places.

Looking for someone's fingers to cover up all the spaces,

Within every space on my hand.

But I will wait,

Because I know what I deserve,

And it's not you.

Luck Ran Up

People can say the right things to take your breath away,

People may give you attention you crave and say they will stay.

But, if you sit back and think,

Loyalty stays,

And love stays,

Love does not change,

People change.

People are confused with love and lust,

To the point their mind is corrupt,

Someone wants to treat them right, so they take that up,

Get stuck up,

And end up leaving the one that cares and love them to downgrade,

Then they wonder if they luck ran up.

Don't Slip or Let Go

It's funny, how people are,

They say one thing and mean another,

They wonder why you're so hard to get because the world is so cold,

The world puts a great burden on your shoulders, and you feel like a lost soul,

Don't slip or let go,

Into the cold world,

Don't lose your happiness,

Don't lose your soul,

Because even when nobody else sees it,

You have a heart of gold,

I'm sorry the world did this to you,

They say the world will change you,

But you never thought in this way.

But a girl with a broken heart will never be the same.

Outside of the box

So, let me get this straight,

The feelings you had for me was fake.

Give or take,

Take…

My breath away,

Is what they all say.

But at the end of the day,

Your mind goes forward then moves back,

Just how she is in the front of your mind and I'm in the back.

That is a guaranteed fact!

You see,

Anyone can make you smile but,

Not everyone cares for you.

Willing to spend their whole life with you,

See,

People don't realize emotions change,

And love is always there,

It's always the same.

You have to be mature enough to see outside the box,

Because when you focus on one thing,

You tend to miss out on everything around it but,

No hard feelings I understand,

Because at the end of the day,

I know what I deserve and that somebody really loves me.

And for me to realize it is to look outside the box.

Nobody

People make time for the people they want,

People hang out with the ones they want,

And people are seen with the ones they want to be seen with.

So, when I realize my place in your life,

That's when I begin to fade out into the background,

And I realize who I am in your life,

A nobody.

In due time it will heal

It seems so clear up close,

But it is like you back up and disappear into the darkness.

All I can see is a reflection,

And reminisce on the song you sung me.

Memories,

Of me and you on the balcony,

It was perfect.

You leaned in for a kiss, but my shyness took over and I just
backed up and smiled,

Stared into your eyes picturing how life would be with you.

But it was like common sense left me,

And it was all emotions clouding my mind and it is like
repetition over and over again.

Same feelings and emotions again,

Just like when I had a lovely night,

It seemed so perfect.

And before I knew it,

He vanished into the night,

And there wasn't a soul in sight,

And I never again saw that smile so bright,

So, in darkness I walked,

And then I waited,

Waited patiently,

Looking for you with a flashlight,

Looking aimlessly,

So now you know why my heart is like steel.

But in due time,

It may heal.

Self-destruct

When you walk by without saying a word is a slap to the face,

Eye contact without hearing your voice is like a dagger to my heart.

It is like I can't focus, and my mind scrambles up,

Someone pats me on my shoulder and says, "baby don't lose yourself."

But I feel like I don't know what to do with myself,

Feels like I am going to self-destruct,

Give up,

Maybe my luck is running up,

Up chuck,

Baby girl don't lose yourself,

Baby girl can you hear me talking to you?

What the world has to say is deaf to my ears,

I wish you was close but,

I wish you wasn't so near.

I wish you were far away but,

You are too far away.

I am a paradox,

I like when time goes by fast but,

I don't want my time to run out,

I want to know everything about you but,

Not too much.

Time is ticking,

I might self-destruct.

I can't do it

I can't do it.

You see,

My heart says one thing and my mind says another.

But it is whatever,

Because we say if it is real,

It wouldn't fade.

But one day you was right beside me,

And the next you went away then it happened again.

And sadly again but,

I remember a little back then,

You was the one who caught my attention and my heart but,

The constant back and forth is a little too much.

And I see myself with you mentally,

But actually, now I see differently.

Words become scrambled and then I choke up,

The picture was painted perfectly and I wasn't in it.

It was like,

I was fading into the background.

Funny how that sounds,

Because you say one thing but do another.

It was as if I was a part of the crowd,

And she's on the front stage with you.

And every time I would hear an "I miss you",

Shortly after, I get a "I can't be with you",

Or "I can't be a part of your life."

Something along those lines,

And I simply just endure the pain,

I mean,

There is nothing else to do,

Not a fan of the blame game,

But seeing you with somebody else,

It was like a knife to the chest.

But I must correct myself,

Because,

There is nothing really, I can do but be in the crowd,

While you are on the front stage with her,

You are probably thinking I am talking about you,

Yes, I am talking about you.

I don't think I can do this back and forth thing anymore.

I guess I have to keep praying and breathing to see what life has in store.

So, if it is real,

It will not fade.

But if I am second choice,

I will make them change.

I just want to be close

I want to know your thoughts,

I want to know every emotion,

I want to know how you feel in your soul,

I want to capture every memory as if it was taken by a camera so that I can bring it back to my remembrance.

I want to grow old with you,

And just hear all the stories of where we were and how we are now.

I want to have you dear to my heart,

Never apart.

I want to be fully naked with you,

Not meaning taking my clothes off for you,

But allowing you to know every little thing about me,

And I know every little thing about you.

I just want to be close to you.

Calamity

It's like calamity,

Chasing after me,

Are you after me?

It said yes gladly,

It's in the back of me,

Chasing me,

Trying to break me,

Trying to shake me,

But lately,

I was chasing you.

But you was in a disguise,

Dressed up so fine.

I just had to make you mine but in due time,

I was wrong.

Had me singing love songs,

I asked myself what I did wrong.

Felt like glee when I heard a love song,

I always sing a long,

But here's a thought,

Take a shot or a chance,

But I wish I would have gave up the chance and give it to Dan,

Got me rhyming like Sam I am,

You got me in your trap so I'm sinking in quick sand,

Didn't even lend a hand,

So you ran away and hid on new land.

But when I got myself together,

You came around and said whatever.

So I'm back,

To what I said before,

It all started when I opened up that door,

It's like calamity chasing after me,

Are you after me?

It said yes gladly,

It's in the back of me,

Chasing me,

Trying to break me,

Trying to shake me,

But lately,

I was chasing you but,

You were in a disguise but this time,

I see right through you,

So, this time,

I won't waste my time on you.

In a Daze

Watching the sunset,

Moonlight picnics,

Taking walks on the beach,

Being with you,

That's where I want to be.

In your arms,

Looking you in your eyes,

Watching your face glow,

Being with you.

The world should know,

Despite all the anger,

Despite all the pain,

My love for you will always be the same,

Dear to my heart,

Near or apart,

Are lives together soon will start.

Going Insane

Painful thought,

Dreadful memories,

What is to be,

Is really not to be,

In my heart,

I feel emptiness,

Inside my mind,

I feel insane,

I have to tell myself,

It's all in my brain.

Telling me what to want,

Telling me how to feel,

The world around me seems so still,

I feel like I am floating above it all.

Trying to stay focus but my mind won't let me,

Constantly having turmoil internally,

Time is flying by fast,

The world is spinning around you then,

SPLAT!

It becomes silent,

As the world around you gets quiet,

The people around you are like giants,

And you are all alone,

Wondering what is next,

I guess you have to wait to see what life projects.

Colorful but Afflicted

When I see you,

I just see a perfect picture.

The more I analyze the photo, the more I see.

A picture so vivid,

Colorful but afflicted.

Feelings inner twine while my heart bleeds,

What to believe?

What is said or what is seen?

So much stuff going through my head,

It all starts in the mind and continues to progress,

You see the problem starts in your mind and makes you go
crazy,

But I wonder if you thought about me lately,

I mean, greatly,

Not just for a minute,

Not just for a thought,

But when I think about you,

It just doesn't stop.

I see you and I see so much,

Guarded on the outside,

But soft to the touch.

Tough to crack,

But I just wait,

Waiting on your guard to break,

Because when you do,

I promise you,

You won't regret it.

I don't care

The worse fear is not knowing,

Not knowing what something could have been and what was meant to be,

The only question there is,

Is why?

Why all the time wasted,

Was it worth it?

The feelings we had disappear,

Were they even real?

Is it my fault I have a heart of steel?

Slowly watching and being aware of my surroundings,

Realizing that I don't care.

Wait, did I just say that?

I don't care or did I really mean that?

A pen and paper recording my response like I really meant that.

But I don't regret you, see,

The past cannot be erased and feelings change in time but,

I waited and God gave me a sign,

And I realized I was fed a bunch of lies.

Time Out

Man,

Quit playing,

You were looking for something real, but I bounced out,

You wanted to show me love but I lashed out,

Did dirt behind my back,

Thought I wouldn't find out?

It's time out,

With the unnecessary pain,

Trying to understand what you heard,

So you reflect back,

Forget that!

Your time ran out,

No more going back to you,

Because I know what you are about.

Why?

Why?

All I can say is,

Why?

Why all of the hurt and pain inside?

Why?

Hold on, let me dry my eyes but,

Why?

I just saw you the other day and you said hey,

You live miles away but you came to see me anyways,

And we talked and laughed but,

Why?

You left without a sign and without words,

Why?

I felt so much pain inside,

Why?

Tried to move on but I still cry,

Why?

I tried to move on but you are still on my mind,

Why?

Listening to slow music while I drive,

Crying my eyes out,

Why?

If I just saw you one more time,

I would just say…

Why?

Dreams I had of you,

Why?

But don't worry,

I'm getting over it day by day,

Little by little,

But still…

You cross my mind from time to time,

Because I constantly ask myself,

Why?

Should I, or Should I Not?

I am constantly contradicting myself,

One minute I want you,

One minute I don't,

One minute I am glad to be with you,

Next minute I am not.

Sometimes I trust you,

At times I am afraid you may hurt me,

I want to show you my romantic side,

But you are not mine, so I fall back.

Sometimes I wonder if your feelings are genuine,

Or are you telling me what I want to hear.

Maybe it is the human in me.

How my mind wanders I may get into trouble,

Or maybe it is because I don't want to get hurt anymore,

I realized everyone will hurt you at some point of time,

Sometimes it is unintentional.

I wish I could read your mind,

And know exactly what you are thinking.

I want to let you into my heart then I tend to pull away,

Because I am so cautious with my heart and with who is worthy
of my vulnerability,

If you truly want me, make it known.

I do not have the time to have someone toy with my emotions.